The development of ESDP instruments during the German EU Presidency and beyond

Stephen Haseler
Jeannette Ladzik

Contents

Notes on the Contributors   v

Acknowledgements   vii

1. **Introduction**   1
   Stephen Haseler and Jeannette Ladzik

2. **The EU as an Actor in Foreign and Security**   5
   Policy: Some Key Features of CFSP in an
   Historical Perspective
   Elfriede Regelsberger

3. **Where we stand: From building Peace in Europe**   21
   to being a Peace-Builder in the World – taking
   stock of the Union's Foreign and Security Policy
   Javier Solana

4. **CFSP after the Footnote Summit**   29
   Annegret Bendiek

5. **The UK and the European Security**   37
   and Defence Policy
   Brendan Donnelly

6. **The Future of European Security and Defence**   45
   Policy: Towards a European Army
   Angelica Schwall-Düren and Fabian Hemker

7. **Hanging together or Hanging separately? The EU3,**   55
   the United States and Iran's Nuclear Quest
   Sebastian Harnisch

8. **Conclusion**   67
   Stephen Haseler and Jeannette Ladzik

Notes on the Contributors

Annegret Bendiek is researcher at the *Stiftung Wissenschaft und Politik*, Berlin.

Brendan Donnelly is Director of the Federal Trust for Education and Research, London.

Sebastian Harnisch is Professor for Political Science at the Ruprecht-Karls-University of Heidelberg.

Stephen Haseler is Director of the Global Policy Institute and Professor of Government at London Metropolitan University.

Fabian Hemker is Angelica Schwall-Düren's parliamentary assistant.

Jeannette Ladzik is researcher at the Global Policy Institute at London Metropolitan University.

Elfriede Regelsberger is Deputy Director of the *Institut für europäische Politik*, Berlin.

Javier Solana is the High Representative for the Common Foreign and Security Policy and Secretary General of the Council of the European Union.

Angelica Schwall-Düren is a Member of the German *Bundestag* and Vice Chairwoman of the SPD in the Bundestag.

Acknowledgements

We would like to thank the executive of the James Madison Trust for its financial support. Without their generous help the research project, which led to this report, could not have been conducted. We would also like to thank Henning Meyer, Ben Eldridge and James Hannah. They provided crucial help in completing this report. And last but not least we would like to express our gratitude to our authors and readers.

Introduction

By Stephen Haseler and Jeannette Ladzik

When Germany took over the six-month rotating presidency of the European Union in the first half of 2007, it was confronted with high hopes and expectations for the outcome of its presidency. These hopes and expectations stemmed from a long list of pressing problems and challenges the EU was facing. Since the lost referenda in France and Luxemburg, the EU has been caught in a vicious circle of public loss of confidence, paralysed institutions and unattainable results. At the same time, the EU and its member states have been confronted with an increasing number of different threats such as terrorism, extremism and organised crime. Accordingly, there has been urgent need to consolidate the Union's internal stability as well as to export stability not only to the Europe's neighbourhood but also to more distant regions.

Given German chairmanship in both the EU and the G8, the country was considered by its EU and international partners to be capable of pushing forward an ambitious agenda and resolving at least some of the pressing problems. Meanwhile, Germany has itself contributed to such expectations as it has in recent years demonstrated its willingness to play a more visible role on the world stage. Indeed in the last couple of years, the long shadow of history seems to have faded and Germany's traditional "culture of restraint" (*Kultur der Zurückhaltung*) has been replaced by more self-confidence and a "normal" foreign policy. Not least the country's readiness to deploy its armed forces without geographic restrictions and to perform the full spectrum of missions as well as its sizeable contributions to the NATO Response Force and to the EU Battlegroups have shown this.

As Germany under Chancellor Merkel has become both pro-European and transatlantic in outlook again, the German presidency was also in a good position to further develop an accentuated role for the European Security and Defence Policy. According to its presidency programme, Berlin's main priorities for ESDP were the stabilisation of the Western Balkan, further development of the EU's operational capacities in the field of crisis management, the strengthening of the civil component of ESDP, better coordination between civil and military instruments and the improvement of the cooperation between the EU and NATO.

Whether Germany was able to achieve its priorities and enhance ESDP instruments will be examined in the framework of this report. The first part of the study deals with the beginning, process and future of the Common Foreign and Security Policy and the European Security and Defence Policy. Elfriede Regelsberger begins by showing how far the EU's project "common foreign policy" has already come when one looks at its beginning – the introduction of "European Political Cooperation". Today thanks to, what Regelsberger calls, "brusselisation" and "socialisation", the EU has got a Common Foreign and Security Policy, whose output in a historical perspective has been impressive. Taking the views of the other partners into account was a novelty in the days of EPC. Today, it is normal to do that before one defines its own position. EU High Representative for CFSP Javier Solana also welcomes the progress of CFSP and ESDP in his article. Especially as regards ESDP operations, he emphasises that where the EU has acted it has succeeded. Yet, there is a great deal more to be done. The EU has to become a peace-builder in the world. Beyond crisis management, the Union should also devote time, energy and resources to address long-term challenges. More precisely, Solana suggests reform of G8 and the UN Security Council. Annegret Bendiek's article deals with the outcome of the June 2007 European Council summit. She scrutinises the CFSP and ESDP provisions, which shall be included in the Reform Treaty, and draws the conclusion that the intended amendments in fact reinforce the intergovernmental character of CFSP and preserve the foreign policy competences of the member states – if not promote a re-nationalisation of the Union's foreign and security policy.

The second and last part of the study analyses the attitudes of the member states towards ESDP and the possible introduction of a *directoire* in ESDP. Brendan Donnelly spells out in his article why the appearance of the Reform Treaty caused difficulties for the new British Prime Minister Gordon Brown. Although Brown has until now refused all suggestions that a referendum on the new treaty needs to be held in the UK, it is uncertain as to whether he will be able and willing to maintain this refusal given the heated polemic about the reform treaty in the British press. Donnelly however points out that the British public is by no means hostile to European efforts in external and defence affairs. Indeed, the British public finds it easier to support the UK playing a role in CFSP and ESDP since both policy areas are run intergovernmentally and the UK can play a leading role in both CFSP and ESDP. A European foreign policy or even more a European security policy without the UK would have little global credibility. The article by Angelica Schwall-Düren and Fabian Hemker tackles the sensitive issue of a European Army by arguing that Germany should support the creation of a European

Army. Germany and the EU have a responsibility to contribute to peace and prosperity in a world that is getting increasingly interdependent. With a European Army, the EU could attain a broader range of political and military instruments and could so increase its weight in the world. According to Schwall-Düren and Hemker, the Battlegroups are not a sufficient means to achieve the Union's security objectives. It seems unlikely that all 27 member states would agree on the build-up of a European Army. If this is the case, Schwall-Düren and Hemker say, it must be realised by way of a "Two-speed-Europe". Sebastian Harnisch' article also touches on the issue of *directoire* in the EU. He examines the efforts of France, Germany and the UK to solve the conflict over Iran's nuclear programme. Their efforts have contributed to the incremental formation of a more unified policy towards Tehran. However, they did not have the negotiation power with all essential positive and negative incentives at their disposal. They needed at least Washington's approval of security assurance for the regime.

The EU as an Actor in Foreign and Security Policy: Some Key Features of CFSP in an Historical Perspective[1]

By Elfriede Regelsberger

Inspired by recent debates, along with the 50th anniversary of the signature of the EC Treaties, this article focuses on the evolution of the "second pillar". Attention will be paid to what started prudently as early as 1970 as an attempt of the then six EC member states in European Political Cooperation (EPC) to prepare the EC "to exercise the responsibilities which to assume in the world is both its duty and a necessity on account of its greater cohesion and its increasingly important role,"[2] and what turned into a legally binding comprehensive commitment of the EU to "define and implement a common foreign and security policy covering all areas" in 1992.[3] Since then the CFSP has constantly[4] been renewed and adjusted to new internal and external challenges, most recently in the 2004 constitutional treaty, which might materialise in the form of the reform treaty 2009 (see Table 1).

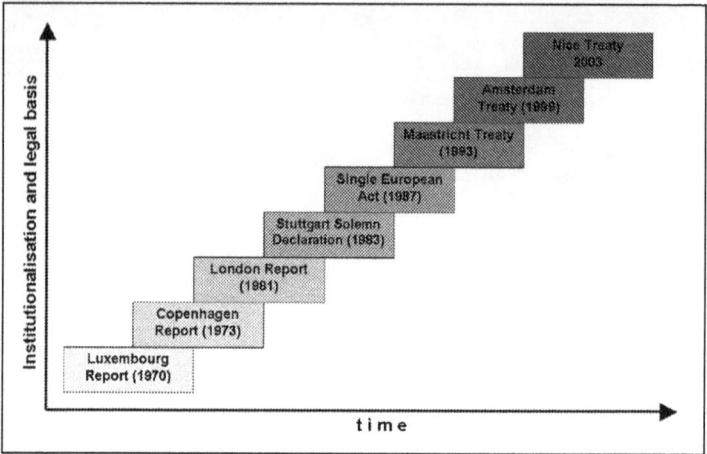

Table 1: CFSP Construction dates

Permanent interest of member states in collective policies

From the beginnings of the EPC until today's CFSP participation in the "club" has become central to the member states. None has ever questioned its membership or left the group. Though the attractiveness of collective foreign policy may be higher among the smaller countries which dispose of only limited diplomatic resources of their own, the bigger ones also wish to profit from CFSP in times of growing interdependencies and globalisation. This "shield" or "umbrella" function of EPC/CFSP has also worked at the domestic political level: it has helped governments to change foreign policy with reference to "constraints" at the European level.[5] Furthermore EPC/CFSP has been helpful on certain occasions when specific national concerns could be made European ones. The UK successfully called for European solidarity in the Falklands War of 1982, Portugal strongly and successfully advocated the issue of East Timor, while Spain did so with regard to Central and Latin America and even France gradually realised that its *domaines reservés* in former colonial Africa could be served through joint European initiatives.

Over time, the general intention of the 1980s that the member states "should seek increasingly to shape events and not merely to react to them"[6] was translated into a legally binding obligation to formulate and implement a common foreign and security policy covering all areas including defence matters. The preservation of peace and security in the world, the protection of human rights and respect for the principles of the UN Charter have been defined as the common objectives of the CFSP. More than in previous times the EU has claimed to be a "power"[7] willing to foster its own values and interests in the world. The 2003 European Security Strategy[8] reaffirmed these ambitions against the background of new challenges such as international terrorism, weapons of mass destruction or failed states.

Contrary to what several observers[9] had assumed with regard to EU enlargement, the "newcomers" in CFSP are well aware of the advantages that membership offers.[10] In fact, no new member state has ever followed the example of *enfant terrible* Greece, which had pains familiarising itself with EPC after its 1981 entry. This negative experience was among the arguments for a more solid basis for EPC. With the 1986 Single European Act, a "legal regime",[11] though in rather general terms, replaced the earlier foreign ministers' reports. The creation of the Single Market, German unification and political changes in Eastern Europe called for something qualitatively new in the late 1980s: the CFSP. Further adaptations became necessary in the course of new external challenges, for example in the Balkans, and due to shortcomings in the existing rules and procedures. The EU's failure to speak with one voice in the Iraq war in 2003 did not produce a standstill in CFSP. On the contrary the conviction grew that another "plateau"[12] had to be reached through legal reform. The somewhat "hidden" constitution building[13] of the 1990s was to be transformed into an "open" one through the Treaty Establishing a Constitution for Europe of 2004 which might be revitalised in its substance during 2007/08.

EPC/CFSP governance at the political and administrative levels
As EPC/CFSP issues are by nature the domain of the foreign ministers and their diplomatic staffs, they have always been the

key players. However, their numbers and the frequency of the meetings of today have nothing more in common with those of the 1970s and 1980s and even throughout the CFSP of the 1990s the growth of actors continued.[14] Similarly the "environment" in which CFSP decisions are prepared and implemented differs from former practices and has implications for the behavioural patterns of those involved.

"Institutionalisation"[15] and "Brusselisation"[16]

As is obvious from Table 2 the institutional set-up has been enlarged.

The rather selective agenda of EPC – the Middle East conflict and the CSCE (today's OSCE) were among the first topics – steadily grew as a result of successful European concertation. The inclusion of foreign policy experts from the national capitals turned out to be vital for the preparations of the ministerial meetings and those of the Political Committee. Apart from new regional and functional topics, security and defence issues gained ground from 1999 and were further accentuated from 2003 with the start of the civilian and military crisis management operations. Furthermore both the legalisation of CFSP decisions and the recourse to Community instruments and finances made it necessary to install specific coordination mechanisms such as the group of RELEX Counsellors.

At the top administrative level, the Political Directors, fundamental changes have taken place. Institutional differentiation followed from the constant overload of the Political Committee and led to the creation of today's Political and Security Committee (PSC) – a new actor designed to be subordinate to the Political Committee in terms of bureaucratic hierarchy but which evolved to the central body in daily CFSP business. In contrast to previous practice when the Political Committee met only once a month or even less in the 1970s, the PSC ambassadors gather twice a week and if necessary more often. What had been unthinkable in EPC days became real from informal   formal establishment

	1970	1986	1993	1996	1999	2000	2001	2003	2004	2005	2006	2007
Heads of State/Government/ European Council												
Foreign Ministers (until 1993; from 1989 onwards meetings on fringe of) Council External Relations												
Foreign + Defence Ministers/ Council External Relations												
Defence Ministers (informal)												
Steering Board EDA (Defence Ministers + others)												
Political Committee (PoCo)												
Political and Security Committee (PSC/ COPS)												
Expert groups/Council working parties												
European Correspondents												
Relex Counsellors												
Nikolaidis Group												
High Representative for the CFSP												
Policy Unit												
Secretariat*												
Special Representatives												
Personal Representatives												
EU Military Committee												
EU Military Staff												
Civil Crisismanagement Committee												
European Defence Agency												
Civ/Mil Cell (Council Secretariat)												
Satellite Centre												
European Security and Defence College												
European Institute for Security Studies												

Table 2: the growth of actors in EPC/CFSP

* In the 1980s a "flying" secretariat existed. From 1986 to 1993 the secretariat was a completely separate "unit" with a "head" inside the Council Secretariat. From 1993 onwards, it was integrated into DG E of the Council Secretariat.

2000 onwards: not only do PSC meetings take place in Brussels but PSC members are located within the member states' representations to the EU. This applies also to the CFSP levels below such as the relatively recent Nikolaidis group whose main task is to prepare the PSC meetings or the RELEX Counsellors responsible for the legal aspects of CFSP decisions and their implications for Community issues.

This trend towards the "Brusselisation" of traditionally capital-based CFSP actors is visible inside the Council framework. The most "revolutionary" change was probably at ministerial level, when the Council of External Relations (an EC organ) became the main CFSP decision-making body. While EPC was marked by the famous and rather inefficient travelling circus of the foreign ministers, from the 1990s they met at the EC sites (Brussels and Luxembourg). The force of events – a credible EU foreign policy calls for a comprehensive interpillar approach – worked in favour of a more unitary institutional set-up. Not surprisingly this process was not tension-free. PSC ambassadors had to find their role vis-à-vis the other body traditionally in charge for the preparations of the Council, the Committee of Permanent Representatives (COREPER).

Commission participation in ESDP-related bodies such as the EU Military Committee raised concern among the governments and competition was strong in areas of overlapping competences such as civilian crisis management. Suspicions were and are strong inside Community circles that the intergovernmental CFSP might interfere with the supranational arena. "Theological" debates promoted separation instead of cooperation and coordination. But even in daily business "everybody sees the need for coordination but nobody wants to be coordinated"' as an insider put it.

This lack of "institutional consistency"[17] slowed down EU decision-making and multiplied the "voices" speaking on the EU's behalf. The creation of the post of a High Representative for the CFSP in 1999 raised considerable concern on the part of the Commissioner for External Relations. Similarly the Policy Unit[18] met with reservations from Commission circles but even inside CFSP and in particular in the Directorate General E of the Council Secretariat suspicions about the "newcomers" existed. Furthermore the numerous Special Representatives worked largely separately from the Commission delegations in third countries. The appointment of E. Fouéré as both Special Representative of the EU to Macedonia and Head of the Commission Delegation in Skopje in 2005 might serve as a model to reduce these frictions. Other recent proposals[19] suggest more intense communication and regular meetings between first and second pillar actors at both political and administrative level but real progress must await the fusion of the posts of High Representative for the CFSP and Commissioner for External Relations.

"Socialisation"

As is well-known the guiding principle for decision-making in both EPC and CFSP has been the consensus rule. Majority voting, though applicable since the Amsterdam Treaty in very rare cases, has remained only on paper. CFSP practitioners argue that the nature and sensitivity of CFSP issues require an atmosphere of negotiations in which each participant is taken on board instead of being excluded and outvoted. The key factor which facilitates consensus building and concrete policy outcomes even in such a large group as the EU-27 has to do with specific behavioural patterns of the participants, the "concertation reflex" or "socialisation". What was a novelty in the days of EPC is normalcy today: taking the views of other partners into account before defining one's own position has become "a naturally done thing" according to insiders.[20] The high degree of institutionalisation and Brusselisation has reinforced this trend of "Europeanising" national foreign policies. The work of the Council Secretariat and the increasingly political functions of the Policy Unit plus the successful performance of the High Representative have also promoted the emergence of an *acquis politique* which is far more than the lowest common denominator. Admittedly history has shown us that socialisation does not work 100 per cent of the time. When the question of peace or war arises and transatlantic relations are at stake, or in situations when issues are already highly politicised at the national level, CFSP decisions are difficult if not impossible to achieve. Also in EU consultations at the United Nations and possibly elsewhere in the world where the positive effects of "Brusselisation" are felt less immediately, the concertation reflex has remained underdeveloped.[21] Here much depends on the skills and personalities of the respective presidency speaking on the EU's behalf and the complexity of the UN proceedings is said to work against greater cohesion. This is not to say that CFSP has failed to produce results in New York. On the contrary and compared to previous periods when unanimous voting was below 50 per cent in the 1970s and even declined in the 1980s, the EU member states today cast collective votes on UN resolutions in around 75-80 per cent of all the submitted texts.[22]

Instruments: growth in quantity and quality
Despite the well-known failures to speak with one voice, the CFSP policy output is impressive both in terms of quantity (breadth of agenda) and quality (differentiation according to substance and instruments).[23] While EPC fell short of instruments other than traditional diplomacy (such as declarations, demarches, Presidency fact-finding missions), CFSP added a set of legal instruments (common strategies, common positions, joint actions) which can take ambitious forms such as the EU's civil and military crisis management operations. The latter[24] require enormous capabilities in term of technical equipment, personal and money and adequate structures for planning and implementing the operations.[25] Though the EU is still far from closing the "expectations-capability gap",[26] progress has been achieved since 2003 in a trial and error process which has not been tension-free, as the controversy over an independent EU Operations Centre or the dispute over arrangements for EU-NATO relations which resulted finally in the "Berlin plus" agreement

revealed.

The progress achieved in ESDP with the "speed of light" – as the High Representative for the CFSP puts it frequently – reflects itself also in the use of the CFSP instruments and in particular those established with the TEU. The growth of CFSP joint actions is largely due to the crisis management operations carried out since 2003 and the need to establish new structures expresses itself in the numerous institutional decisions of the Council and the PSC. Similarly the more frequent use of agreements with third countries has to do with the growing interest of non-EU member states to participate in ESDP missions. As the graph below illustrates, the rise in CFSP acts of "non-territorial subjects" over the past years is also partly ESDP-driven. Other issues of this category refer to non proliferation and to the EU's measures – normally in the form of common positions – to combat international terrorism after 11 September 2001.

The instrument of common positions is also frequently used to define the EU's approach towards third countries or regions outside the immediate neighbourhood, such as the ACP countries, while joint actions usually address relations with the Balkans, the Middle East and more recently Central Asia and the South Caucasian region. The former are also applied in case of sanctions, while the mandates of the Special Representatives – another successful approach to be more operational and present on the ground – are defined through joint actions.

All these activities have financial implications and as such clearly differ from the old, "cheaper" EPC instruments. The financing of the CFSP[27] caused severe controversies between diplomats and Community bodies and in particular the European Parliament since the latter tried to improve its competences inside CFSP through its rights as part of the budgetary authority in the EC. However, even strong intergovernmentalists voted for the application of the Community procedures for the CFSP finances in the Amsterdam Treaty (1997) either because national budgets fell short of money or the government representatives were not aware of the concrete EC mechanisms these rules would entail. Another source of tensions between the Council and European Commission arose from the fact that CFSP expenditure fell constantly short of the policies pursued.[28] Consequently CFSP still has to seek additional funding from other sources of the Community budget which, however, belong to the Commission.

	2001	2003	2005	2006
Joint actions (including implementation decisions)	19	20	42	65
Common positions (including implementation decisions)	20	20	29	29
Agreements with third countries (art. 24 TEU)	2	16	15	16
Decisions on ESDP by PSC	–	–	13	–[1]
Other Council decisions on ESDP	–	–	5	–[2]
Other Council decisions related to CFSP	6	13	10	5
Declarations	196	150	153	148
Demarches	442	606	292	463
Political Dialogue	306	228	134	154
Joint reports from diplomatic missions in third countries	278	391	258	318

Table 3: The use of instruments in CFSP

1 Since these decisions refer normally to the implementation of joint actions and common positions they have been included in those categories already which explains the growth rates there compared to previous years.
2 Since these decisions refer normally to the implementation of joint actions and common positions they have been included in those categories already which explains the growth rates there compared to previous years.

As table 3 illustrates the use of the more "traditional" instruments of collective foreign policy-making has gone down. Nevertheless CFSP declarations may prove to be at least an additional tool to express the views of the EU-27 on a particular issue. Despite the harsh and often unjustified criticism of "mere" declaratory policy, reactions from third parties indicate that even words may have a significance in foreign policy. More than before CFSP declarations today often contain a "conditionality clause", that is in case the addressee aligns with the policy of the EU-27 it may profit from specific EU support (aid, trade concessions, etc) or lose it in case of deviation.

Interventions against the violation of human rights[29] are usually high on the CFSP agenda. They can take very different forms and it seems that the instrument of the diplomatic – and by its nature confidential – demarche has lost importance while meetings in the framework of political dialogues are used more intensively. This holds true for the specific human rights dialogues the EU has established with China, Iran and Russia even though insiders admit that they have produced only "mixed results" so far. But in other regular gatherings between the EU and third countries or regional groupings human rights questions have been addressed more often.[30] Generally political dialogues have served the EU well to "export" its own successful model of integration to other parts of the world (ASEAN; Gulf Cooperation Council) and through them the EU has offered its services as a mediator and partner (as in Central and Latin America, or the Barcelona process). Since this instrument requires excessive preparation inside the EU and involves a great number of participants in case meetings take place in full format (EU-27) adaptations have been made to "economise" the dialogues: to reduce the number of participants (Troika; High Representative), to streamline the agenda, or even to reduce the number of meetings. The fewer dialogues conducted since 2003 (see Table 3) only partly reflects this trend. The massive decrease between 2003 and 2005 has to do with the 2004 enlargement: before accession, the EU briefed future members about the CFSP results in separate dialogue meetings which were then no longer necessary.

In a historical perspective the output of CFSP – and to a lesser extent its precursor EPC – has been impressive. Even though it is difficult view to measure the international impact of CFSP policies, the permanent interest of the EU member states to use CFSP and adapt the framework to new challenges indicates its value, as do the recognition and growing demands for a European foreign and security policy from outside. Imperfect as it may be with regard to cross-pillar coordination, military capabilities and institutional shortcomings such as the rotating presidency, the "phenomenon" of CFSP will remain of high relevance for both the political world and academic research.

Endnotes

1   This paper summarises what the author presented to the UACES Conference on "Reflections on European Integration: 50 Years of the Treaty of Rome", in London, 23-24 March 2007, and is based on earlier work: E. Regelsberger (2004): Die Gemeinsame Außen- und Sicherheitspolitik der EU (GASP), Baden-Baden. The article was first published in CFSP Forum, vol.5, no.4, July 2007.

2   First Report of the Foreign Ministers to the Heads of State and Government of the European Community of 27 October 1970 (Luxembourg Report), point 9.

3   Title V Art.J, Treaty on European Union (Maastricht version).

4   Title V Art.11, Treaty on European Union (Amsterdam version of 1997 and Nice version of 2001).

5   For example, Germany preferred to use EPC to adapt its Middle East policy in the 1970s. For the "shield effect" in the UN framework see Smith, Karen (2006): "Speaking with One Voice? European Union Co-ordination on Human Rights Issues at the United Nations", Journal of Common Market Studies, vol. 44, no. 1.

6   Report on European Political Cooperation, 13 October 1981 (London Report).

7   This was the wording of the 2001 Laaken Declaration of the European Council which kicked off the European Convention.

8   Designed by the High Representative for the CFSP and adopted by the European Council in December 2003.

9   See CFSP Forum, vol. 3, no. 3, May 2005.

10 See Regelsberger, Elfriede, Wolfgang Wessels (2004): "The Evolution of the Common Foreign and Security Policy. A Case for an Imperfect Ratched Fusion", in: Verdun, A., O. Croci (eds): Institutional and Policy-making Challenges to the European Union in the Wake of

Eastern Enlargement, Manchester.

11 See Smith, Michael E. (2004): Europe's Foreign and Security Policy: The Institutionalization of Cooperation, Cambridge.

12 This notion was introduced to describe the various stages of the EPC. See Hill, Christopher, William Wallace (1979): "Diplomatic Trends in the European Community", International Affairs, pp. 47-66; Regelsberger, Elfriede (1988): "EPC in the Eighties: A Qualitative Leap Forward?", in: Pijpers, Alfred, Elfriede Regelsberger, Wolfgang Wessels (ed): European Political Cooperation in the 1980s. A Common Foreign Policy for Western Europe?. Another term used was "periods"; see Nuttall,Simon (1997): "Two Decades of EPC Performance", in: Regelsberger, Elfriede, Philippe de Schoutheete, Wolfgang Wessels (eds): Foreign Policy of the European Union. From EPC to CFSP and Beyond.

13 See Regelsberger, Elfriede, Wolfgang Wessels (2004): "The Evolution of the Common Foreign and Security Policy. A Case for an Imperfect Ratched Fusion", in: Verdun, A., O. Croci (eds): Institutional and Policy-making Challenges to the European Union in the Wake of Eastern Enlargement, Manchester.

14 For an overview see Duke, Simon, Sophie Vanhoonacker (2006): "Administrative Governance in the CFSP: Development and Practice", European Foreign Affairs Review, no.11.

15 See Smith, Michael E. (2004): Europe's Foreign and Security Policy: The Institutionalization of Cooperation, Cambridge.

16 Among the first: Allen, David (1997): "Who speaks for Europe?", in: Petersen, John, Helen Sjursen (eds): A Common Foreign Policy for Western Europe? Competing Visions of CFSP, London.

17 See Nuttall, Simon (2005): "Coherence and Consistency", in: Hill, Christopher, Michael Smith (eds): International Relations and the European Union, Oxford.

18 Its official name in the 1997 Amsterdam Treaty – Policy Planning and Early Warning Unit – is no longer used since it does not correspond to its factual role.

19 European Commission (2006): "Europe in the World – Some Practical Proposals for Greater Coherence, Effectiveness and Visibility", COM 278 final; Presidency Conclusions, European

Council, 15/16 June 2006, Doc. 10633/06 CONCL 2.

20 See Juncos, Ana, Karolina Pomorska (2006): "Playing the Brussels Game: Strategic Socialisation in the CFSP Council Working Groups", European Online Papers, vol. 10.

21 See Smith, Karen (2006): "Speaking with One Voice? European Union Co-ordination on Human Rights Issues at the United Nations", Journal of Common Market Studies, vol. 44, no. 1.

22 See Sucharipa, E. (2003): „Die Gemeinsame Außen- und Sicherheitspolitik (GASP) der Europäischen Union im Rahmen der Vereinten Nationen", in: Liber Amicorum Tono Eitel, Max Planck Institut Heidelberg. Research in the field of the UN is underdeveloped at present.

23 For further details see "Annual report from the Council to the European Parliament on the main aspects and basic choices of CFSP, including the financial implications for the general budget of the European Communities", Doc. 10314/06 PESC 562 FIN 234 PE 192.

24 As for first assessments see among others: Nowak, Agnieszka (2006): "Civilian Crisis Management: The EU Way", Chaillot Paper, no. 90, Paris EU ISS; Ehrhart, Hans-Georg (2007): "EUFOR RD Congo: a preliminary assessment", European Security Review, no.32, Brussels; Gourlay, Catriona, et al. (2006): "Civilian Crisis Management: The EU Way", Chaillot Paper, no. 90, Paris EU ISS.

25 See Howorth, Jolyon (2005): "From Security to Defence: the Evolution of the CFSP", in: Hill, Christopher, Michael Smith (eds); International Relations and the European Union, Oxford.

26 Introduced by: Hill, Christopher (1994): "The Capability-Expectations Gap, or Conceptualizing Europe's International Role", in: Bulmer, Simon, Andrew Scott (eds): Economic and Political Integration in Europe, Oxford.

27 The funding of CFSP measures having military or defence implications is excluded from the Community budget (art. 28 TEU) and depends on national contributions.

28 In 2005 the CFSP budget was only around 62 million. For the period 2007-13 a rise from 150 to 340 million is foreseen, not least because of the insistence of the High Representative. Bendiek, Annegret (2006): "The financing of the CFSP/ESDP: "There is a

democratic deficit problem"", CFSP Forum, vol.6, no.4.

29 More information is available through the annual Council reports on the human rights situation.

30 See, for example, during the 2007 German Presidency the ministerial meeting between the EU and ASEAN concerning the issue of Burma.

Where we Stand: From building peace in Europe to being a peace-builder in the world – taking stock of the Union's foreign and security policy

By Javier Solana

Early this year, the European Union celebrated its 50th birthday. In these 50 years, Europe has been transformed. A continent plagued by wars and confrontations has developed into a community of peace, democracy and prosperity. We have stopped killing each other and starting to work together.

This did not happen by itself. We built strong institutions and a community of law to make the integration process withstand the ebb and flow of political moods and clashes of personalities. We have learned, the hard way, that peace and stability require common rules and institutions, non-stop negotiations and a sense of compromise. We have also not abolished nations, states or sovereignty, but changed their nature. Sovereignty is now expressed not by an army at the frontier but by a seat at the table.

These successes are worth cherishing. But there is a great deal more to be done. In many ways the peaceful unification of our continent has been our great achievement. To act as a credible force for good is now our main challenge. From a continental agenda, we should move to a global agenda. From building peace in Europe to peace-builder in the world.

With respect to Europe's global role, there is much that we have already achieved. We have expanded our capacity to respond to crises in real time – and not just send out a communiqué two weeks after the event. We have developed sophisticated crisis management concepts – bringing together civilian and military instruments. We have forged a common strategic culture – enabling us to respond early, rapidly and where necessary, robustly when a new crisis erupts. In short, there is a European way of looking at international problems and a shared sense doctrine on how to solve them.

In the years ahead, we will have to sharpen our crisis management performance in a more demanding security environment. But, first, let me sketch our present ESDP operations.

ESDP in practice: Operations
Last year, the European Union conducted 10 operations with around 10 000 men and women serving in them. The global reach and the scope of these different operations is striking. Across three continents, they cover the spectrum from "pure" military operations – through security-sector reform and institution building – to police and rule-of-law missions. And their impact is significant. From Aceh to Rafah, and from Kinshasa to Sarajevo, the EU is providing the "key enablers" for peace and stability.

- In the Democratic Republic of Congo (DRC), a country which has seen three million of its citizens killed in a five-year conflict, we acted decisively to ensure that the electoral process enabled the peaceful transition to a democratically elected government.
- In Aceh, the EU moved quickly with its Association of South East Asian Nations (ASEAN) partners to capitalise on their post-Tsunami desire for peace and opportunity.

- In Rafah, we acted two weeks after an Israeli and Palestinian request to enable the opening of the border crossing point. By working alongside Israelis and Palestinians, we provide the only safety valve for the pressure cooker that is Gaza.
- In the West Bank, in Kinshasa, in Darfur and in Bosnia and Herzegovina we mentor, monitor and support the local police.
- Also in Bosnia and Herzegovina our military force, run under the Berlin Plus arrangements, continues to ensure a safe and secure environment.
- We also have security-sector reform and rule-of-law training missions in the DRC and Iraq respectively.
- Most recently, we have launched our police mission in Afghanistan. Working together closely with the local police, we try to ensure that Afghan communities enjoy the benefits of increased security and to support local authorities in taking responsibility for law and order.

And the demand on the EU is increasing. This year, we will add to these responsibilities the conduct of a police and rule-of-law mission in Kosovo. In Kosovo, we will launch our largest ever civilian mission. It is already clear that this mission will form a critical part of the agenda for ESDP this year and beyond. It is also right that we take on a greater operational role in our "backyard" and our planning for this mission is well under way.

Combined, these operations represent a significant engagement by the EU on the key stability challenges. The EU has responded to the demands of its Member States, to the demands of countries in crisis and to the calls for help from the UN. And we had to respond to the changing world, even before our doctrines and structures had caught up completely.

Each crisis threw up its own set of different and unpredicted requirements: some required a rapid, robust military response to the centre of Africa, some a rapid deployment of police and border monitors to a Middle East hotspot. Some, such as Aceh, support to AMIS and EUSEC (EU mission to provide advice and assistance for security sector reform in the Democratic Republic of Congo) required a different mix of civilian and military instruments.

And where we have acted we have succeeded. We have helped governments take forward their peace processes and we have helped to make those processes more sustainable by strengthening their institutions. Most of all, although much remains to be done, of course, in all of these places, we have improved the lives of people and given them hope.

Beyond this, let us look at how ESDP has changed our Union, and our wider impact on the world. CFSP has changed our Union and how we interact with the world. It is a vital, visible and effective part of our daily lives. Imagine a world where there were no unified positions of the EU: on Iran, on the Middle East, on Africa, on climate change and on the Doha Round?

It is true that the business of reaching unified positions is sometimes painful. But this is just a fraction of the pain felt when a common position is not reached. And, when we do not agree, the pain is not just felt by ourselves, but often far beyond. Fortunately, this is not often the case.

ESDP and CFSP: Beyond crisis-management

CFSP strengthens the effectiveness of ESDP. The political framework gives our operations clear objectives and deep support. And ESDP has made CFSP more credible, and it has given our dialogue with third countries strength.

It makes multilateralism effective, and it helps shape the thinking of others. It means we can act together to address a range of different issues that concern us. Our unity, our influence and our action benefits us, of course. But it also serves many others. And, actually, it is often easier for us to act together than alone. Solidarity and shared political objectives are good force generators, and our collective weight counts. It is also true that in many cases Member States can no longer act alone to any great effect.

Now, can you imagine a Europe that is just a Europe of dialogue and common positions and no action? Not for many people in Africa, the Middle East and the Balkans – who have benefited from our action. And not for many citizens of our own countries or for our many partners around the world who have been calling for more European action and not less.

However, all this risks to make us a victim of our success. We are called upon to undertake more missions and in more difficult circumstances. In Africa or in Asia, on nuclear issues, man-made or natural disasters – we are being solicited. And we have no choice but to be ready and to say "Yes". Therefore, we need to make sure we are structured and staffed to meet all these different challenges.

A global agenda

However, regarding the global agenda, there is much more. Beyond crisis-management, we will have to devote time, energy and resources to also address longer-term challenges. And perhaps the most important of these is to safeguard the capacity of the global system. If truth be told, the global system is in a poor shape.

What we are seeing is that there is a growing mismatch between our security and economics, which are increasingly global in nature, and our politics which often remain national.

Few today would dispute that in a global, interdependent world, solutions to problems will have to be forged at a global level. But the gap between this demand for "global governance" and its supply is growing. Instead the multilateral system is under severe stress.

Some of the "old regimes" on issues such as non-proliferation are suffering from political polarisation, growing distrust and hence a sense of malaise. On issues that have shot to the top of the agenda more recently, such as migration or organised crime, attempts to build regimes, rules and institutions are still incomplete.

Therefore, one key task for Europe for the next 50 years is to protect and develop a system of strong institutions able to tackle the problems of a new age; and to build a rules-based international order with the rules that will help us navigate the choppy waters ahead.

We will have to do so at when the world is moving to a system of continents. Europeans will only be able to project and protect their interests if are united.

New heavyweights and new bargains

But we will also need to make space at the top table. Take the G-8. At present it does not really work effectively. To become more effective, it needs to become more representative and that means changing its membership.

Why not make it a G-10 in which the ten major countries are represented based on a composite index of international weight (GDP, aid, soldiers and civilians deployed on peace support missions)? This would not only bring China and India in but also keep some current members on their toes.

Equally we should make space for the new heavyweights at the UN Security Council. In turn, the new powers should keep in mind that with greater global influence come greater responsibilities too. To strengthen regional co-operation, could we have (semi)-permanent seats at the UNSC for the Great Powers but also for regional organisations?

I am convinced that we need stronger regional organisations: the African Union, ASEAN, Latin American structures. I also wonder whether – in the long run – the Middle East region will remain the big exception: over-armed, under-institutionalised and rife with tensions.

Then we will need to develop new bargains. On the environment and climate change. Or on forms of dialogues between cultures.

Sometimes we also need to be more serious about upholding our side of the old bargain. Non-proliferation is a good example. If we want to be credible on preventing the spread of weapons of mass destruction (WMD), we have to take the disarmament side and technology transfer sides of the bargain more seriously.

In addition, the multilateral system cannot only address our immediate concerns. When we talk about non-proliferation we mostly mean WMD. But for many African or Asian leaders the most urgent proliferation problem is that of small arms and light weapons.

Above all, we need to re-learn that the biggest shift in history came when we extended the rule of law. First within states and now, gradually, also among them. This gradual extension of the international rule of law has provided enormous benefits: taming the passion of states but also providing a legal framework to guide many aspects of human inter-actions at a global level.

We should step up what we are already doing. Regionally – most strikingly in Europe. But also globally on some aspects of international life. See the WTO dispute settlement system, or the International Criminal Court. We have to work hard to extend the geographic and functional reach of the international legal system.

In short, to organise our globalised world, we need to share power (with new players); re-think power (beyond the state paradigm) and tame power (extend the rule of law internationally).

International legitimacy revisited

The system of global governance needs to be made more effective. It also needs to be more legitimate. One big problem is that we all know that we live in a globalized world. But our politics remain local or national.

This is a problem for those, like me, who are convinced that the world needs more global-level, multilateral co-operation. For I am also a democrat in believing that power has to be accountable.

So the question becomes: how do you make global governance more effective while making it also democratically accountable?

A key benefit of acting multilaterally is legitimacy which in turns enhances effectiveness. As indicated earlier, this means bringing in new centres of power. But legitimacy also means bringing our publics along. If decisions are increasingly taken at the international level, people have to see these as legitimate.

Therefore, we have two imperatives: to create greater effectiveness in global governance but also to uphold democratic legitimacy. To do so is difficult. It requires new ideas and a sense of compromise. But I really see no real alternative.

Let me end with a quote from Jean Jacques Rousseau, from The Social Contract, now that we are talking about a global social contract.

"The strongest is never strong enough to be always the master, unless he transforms strength into right and obedience into duty."

As new powers emerge and new issues call for our engagement, Europe will have to apply itself to the task of promoting the emergence of an new international order. An international order which is based on clear rules and strong institutions.

A failure to do take up this task would mean having to live in a world shaped by and for others; a world which would be more unstable and more unjust.

CFSP after the Footnote Summit

By Annegret Bendiek[1]

At the European Council summit in June 2007 the heads of state and government agreed to create the office of a High Representative of the Union for Foreign Affairs and Security Policy and an External Action Service. Yet, at the same time several of the 23 footnotes of the Presidency Conclusion stressed that neither the responsibilities of the member states for their foreign policy nor of their national representation in third countries and international organisations shall be affected in the future. Pro-integrationists like Luxemburg and Italy criticised the outcome of the summit since it does not foresee to transfer further foreign and security policy competences to the EU-level.

The EU leaders agreed on a reform of the constitutional treaty at their summit in June 2007. The Portuguese EU Presidency plans to convene an Intergovernmental Conference (IGC) which on the basis of the summit's political agreement will decide concrete revisions of the existing treaties by autumn 2007. At the summit, the then incumbent British Prime Minister Tony Blair demanded both to reconsider the 2004 IGC's foreign policy conclusions and to bring them in line with a stronger intergovernmental co-operation. The member states agreed on the one hand that the future IGC shall decide not to install the office of a European Foreign Minister but the office of a High Representative of the Union for Foreign Affairs and Security Policy who should be at the same time Vice-President of the European Commission and External Relations Commissioner. The High Representative shall have the right of initiative and permanently preside over the External Relations Council. He/she will be assisted by a European diplomatic service which brings together officials from EU institutions and staff seconded from the diplomatic services of the member states. On the other hand, the EU leaders underlined that the reform treaty must guarantee that the foreign and security policy responsibilities of the member states will not be prejudiced. It shall therefore be stressed that the Union will only act within the boundaries of the competences conferred upon it by the member states in the treaties.

Only a new title?
For everyday language the title "High Representative of the Union for Foreign Affairs and Security Policy" can rarely be used. Indeed, fundamental sovereignty reservations and reluctance to transfer foreign policy competences to the EU are behind the new title (see footnote in Presidency Conclusions – Brussels, 21/22 June 2007).

In principle, the competences agreed in the 2004 IGC will be implemented in the existing treaties by the reform treaty. In Title V of the existing Treaty on the European Union (TEU) – General Provisions on the Union's external action and specific Provisions on the Common Foreign and Security Policy – the first chapter on the principles and objectives of the Union's external action will be replaced by a new text in the Reform Treaty (see box 1).

In Article 11, insertion of a paragraph 1 reading as follows (the current text of paragraph 1 being deleted):
"1. The Union's competence in matters of common foreign and security policy shall cover all areas of foreign policy and all questions relating to the Union's security, including the progressive framing of a common defence policy that might lead to a common defence. The common foreign and security policy is subject to specific procedures. It shall be defined and implemented by the European Council and the Council acting unanimously, except where the Treaties provide otherwise. The adoption of legislative acts shall be excluded. The common foreign and security policy shall be put into effect by the High Representative of the Union for Foreign Affairs and Security Policy and by Member States, in accordance with the Treaties. The specific role of the European Parliament and of the Commission in this area is defined by the Treaties. The Court of Justice of the European Union shall not have jurisdiction with respect to these provisions, with the exception of its jurisdiction to monitor the compliance with Article [III-308] and to review the legality of certain decisions as provided for by Article [III-376, second subparagraph]."

Box 1: Title V "General provisions on the Union's external action and specific provisions on the Common Foreign and Security Policy"

In the new paragraph the special role of the European Council in setting the EU's external relations is defined. By explicitly saying that the European Council (heads of state and government) and the Council of the European Union (General Affairs Council) unanimously determine and carry out the Common Foreign and Security Policy (CFSP) the competency of the future High Representative is clearly limited. Moreover considering external representation, the division of labour between the High Representative of the Union – who at the same time is

Commissioner for External Relations and Vice-President of the Commission – the President of the European Council and the President of the Commission regarding external representation remains unclear. Not least therefore, it is foreseeable that on administrative level the External Action Service will become divided alongside institutional separation lines between Council and Commission depending on the external competences so that one part of the Service will work for the Council whilst the other one works for the Commission. For example, while the Council will continue to conduct the political dialogue within the framework of the European Neighbourhood Policy, the Commission will shape external trade relations. The European Security and Defence Policy will keep its institutional special status and therefore will not become a work sector within the new External Action Service.

A second new chapter in Title V of the existing TEU contains the provisions on CFSP as modified in the 2004 IGC, including the External Action Service and permanent structured cooperation in the field of defence. Also, there will be a specific legal basis on personal data protection in the CFSP area in order to meet the concerns that the corresponding national legal bases remain unaffected.

In addition to the new procedures of Title V, the IGC shall agree on a declaration, which stresses the following principles for CFSP:

- The provisions in the Treaty on European Union covering CFSP, including the creation of the High Representative of the Union for Foreign Affairs and Security Policy and the establishment of an External Action Service, "do not affect the responsibilities of the member states, as they currently exist, for the formulation and conduct of their foreign policy nor of their national representation in third countries and international organisations."
- The provisions governing the European Security and Defence Policy "do not prejudice the specific character of the security and defence policy of the member states."

- The EU and its member states "will remain bound by the provisions of the Charter of the United Nations" and, in particular, by the resolutions of the Security Council.
- The Commission will not be granted new powers in CFSP to initiate decisions; also the external role of the European Parliament will not be increased.

The IGC shall furthermore decide that the EU will get "legal personality". This could in the future enhance the EU's role when international agreements will be concluded or questions of territorial recognition are concerned. At the same time, the IGC shall make sure that the EU will not be authorised to act beyond the competences conferred upon it by the member states. In the final provisions, the possibility of voluntary withdrawal from the EU is foreseen. Every applicant state will be obliged to respect the criteria for membership as determined by the European Council and furthermore to promote the values of the Union. This could raise the hurdle for EU membership.

In the EC Treaty on the functioning of the EU a stipulation important for the EU's foreign policy will be added: the EU can only join the European Court of Human Rights when the Council unanimously decided so. The member states need to ratify this decision.

"Flexible Integration" and "enhanced cooperation"
The provisions on "flexible integration" or "enhanced cooperation" do not change the fact that national sovereignty instead of CFSP has been protected in the EU's external relations. The flexibility clause allows the Union to act if the Council unanimously agrees. Yet, this instrument can still not be applied to the objectives of CFSP as it was already decided at the 2004 IGC. Therefore, without altering the treaty the member states are not allowed to declare CFSP as community competence even when they have reached a unanimous decision. Hence, unanimity is still required for decisions relating to CFSP; for the time being qualified majority voting will not be

extended to the CFSP area. Moreover, the adoption of legislative acts will not be introduced in CFSP. Decisions covering the Union's external relations are therefore rarely legally binding. The non-implementation of the flexibility clause in CFSP can be explained by the negative foreign policy experience of the Iraq crisis and the risk of splitting Europe's foreign policy.

"Enhanced cooperation" in CFSP in its existing form cannot make up for the non-application of the flexibility clause. At the 2004 IGC, it was agreed that the minimum number of member states required for launching an enhanced cooperation will be nine. This rule shall be, as it stands, introduced into the reform treaty (Title IV new). The EU member states simply lack the political will to allow an enhanced cooperation with less than nine member states on the basis of the TEU. The experience however has shown that it is unrealistic to get together nine countries which agree to form a foreign policy avant-garde group. As a result of this rule, it will become rather unlikely that on the basis of the reform treaty a "Core Europe" in the area of foreign policy will emerge. Outside of the treaty regulations, so-called ad-hoc groups or coalitions of the willing, which consist of less than 9 members, have for some time now been part to Europe's foreign and security policy reality.

Incremental advancement

The intended amendments are in fact institutional reforms, which just reinforce the intergovernmental character of CFSP and preserve the foreign policy competences of the member states – if not promote a re-nationalisation of the Union's foreign and security policy: vague authorities of the High Representative, explicit concessions to the European Council and the member states in the form of decision-making and implementation of decisions, the declaration on member states' foreign policy sovereignty, the non-application of the flexibility clause and the limited validity of enhanced cooperation do not add to a strengthening of CFSP. The question is whether one can press ahead with the "europeanisation" of CFSP beyond institutional reforms and in the framework of a "weak constitutionalisation", which does not require an alteration of treaty provisions. When considering the annexes of the Presidency Conclusion from June 2007, two ways of a so-called incremental advancement of European politics become apparent. Both would allow for a deepening of CFSP in geographic as well as in conceptual dimension without having to amend the treaties:

a) Geographic dimension
The Presidency Progress Report on the European Neighbourhood Policy (ENP), the Black Sea Synergy Initiative and the EU Strategy on Central Asia show that the EU geographically extends its external relations and so, establishes an Energy Foreign Policy without altering the TEU. In order to achieve independence from Russian energy the EU has intensified its relationship to Norway and moreover to the 16 ENP partner countries and Central Asian countries.

b) Conceptual dimension
The 2007 Presidency Conclusion's annexes include the Council Conclusions on Extending and Enhancing the Global Approach to Migration, the Presidency Report on ESDP and the Presidency report on EU activities in the framework of prevention, including implementation of the EU Programme for the Prevention of Violent Conflicts. In these reports, the Union commits itself to contribute to effective multilateralism and to improve the link between internal and external as well as civil and military instruments. For instance, when the EU conducted a military operation in the Democratic Republic of the Congo a joint comprehensive concept for the reform of the security sector in the Congo was elaborated in order to attain coherence between the civil and military means of the Commission and the Council. A better attunement of internal and external as well as civil and military instruments could lead to a centralisation of Europe's foreign and security policy.

The review of the 2008 EU budget will have to show whether development of CFSP can not only be driven further on paper but financially: namely if it is decided to increase the EU budget. In the light of the 21st century's foreign policy realities, the EU must better communicate its politics to its citizens in order to maintain the high CFSP's approval rating and so provide financial support for CFSP.

Endnote

1   The article is a translation of a German article by Annegret Bendiek, which was first published in SWP-Aktuell 42 under the title "GASP nach dem Fußnotengipfel".

The UK and the European Security and Defence Policy

By Brendan Donnelly

The German Presidency of the European Union in the first half of 2007 will rightly be remembered for its success in relaunching the process of the Union's institutional reform. This process had been immobilised by the outcomes of the French and Dutch referendums in 2005, when the European Constitutional Treaty was rejected by clear majorities in both countries. The detailed mandate for a new "Reform Treaty" agreed by the European Council in June 2007 offers however a clear opportunity for the Union to emerge from the political and institutional impasse of the past two years. If the new Treaty is signed and ratified within the timetable adopted by the European Council, a number of its provisions will have important implications for the developing European Security and Defence Policy. The enhanced role of the Union's High Representative for External Affairs and the innovative concept of "structured co-operation" in the military field are two central elements of the abandoned Constitutional Treaty which have been retained in the "Reform Treaty" and which will certainly help shape if implemented both the day to day and long-term workings of ESDP.

Reactions to the new Treaty in the United Kingdom have been confused and contrasting. Mr. Blair, who signed the European Constitutional Treaty in 2004, spent the last days of his premiership negotiating to protect the United Kingdom from its supposed inadequacies. Having secured this "protection" for the United Kingdom, he now vehemently asserts that there is no case for his successor, Gordon Brown, to hold a referendum on what is now simply an amending treaty, and not a constitutional document. Mr. Brown in his turn is assaulted by critics claiming, with much justice, that the contents of the new treaty are very similar to the essential contents of the Constitutional Treaty. If that treaty merited a referendum in the United Kingdom, so their argument runs, then the new treaty should also be subjected to a popular vote. Mr. Brown has until now refused all suggestions of a referendum on European institutional questions. Commentators are divided as to whether he will be able and willing to maintain this refusal indefinitely.

Interestingly, in all the heated British polemic about the "Reform Treaty" the role of the High Commissioner has figured only marginally, and the matter of "structured co-operation" hardly at all. Much more attention has figured on the extension of qualified majority voting (both actual and potential) envisaged in the treaty, the consolidated legal personality of the Union and the semi-permanent Presidency of the European Council. This structure of the debate is illuminating. British public and political opinion is by no means hostile to common European efforts in external and defence affairs. The argument that no individual European country can defend or advance its interests effectively alone in the wider world is one which has as much resonance in the United Kingdom as it does in other European countries. British electors join their German, French and other European counterparts in recognising that on many external issues, such as climate change, energy security, the Middle East, international terrorism and the role of multilateral institutions, there are specific and recognisable European interests which need to be pursued communally on the international stage. There are, however, two specifically British components to the way in which these matters are debated in the United Kingdom. British public and political opinion finds it much easier for the United Kingdom to play a relatively full and constructive role in both CFSP and ESDP because these policy areas are run inter-governmentally and because both are policy areas in which the United Kingdom can play a leading, even predominant role. These considerations colour even more profoundly the British approach to ESDP than to CFSP.

From the very beginning of British membership in the European Community, British attitudes towards the central European institutions and the integrative philosophy which they represent have always been coloured by suspicion and even outright hostility. While for the great majority of continental European opinion, such institutions as the European Commission, the European Parliament and the European Court of Justice are seen as central to the political project which is the European Union, no such consensus exists within the United Kingdom. Even the political nature of the integration sought by the Union is routinely denied or rejected by British commentators. The European institutions which (not wrongly) are seen as pillars of this political integration are regarded by wide segments of British opinion as wholly lacking in autonomous legitimacy, as anachronistic remnants of an always unrealistic aspiration to create a "country called Europe." With the single exception of Edward Heath, no British Prime Minister has since Britain joined the European Union been willing to explain in sympathetic terms to the British electorate the wholly legitimate and politically central role of the autonomous European institutions in the organisation which the United Kingdom joined in 1973. Some British Prime Ministers, for example Mr. Blair, no doubt feared that any such attempts at political education on their part might be counter-productive, fuelling British popular fears of a European "superstate." The increasingly frenetic and Eurosceptic tone of public debate on European issues in the United Kingdom over the past decade suggests that Mr. Blair's reticence may itself have had the counter-productive effects which he feared might arise from a more robust public advocacy of the realities which underlie the European Union. It has been plausibly reported recently that the British Foreign Office has been instructed internally and externally never in future to use the phrase "European integration" when referring to the European Union, but rather always to speak of "European co-operation." Sometimes, the current British government likes to claim that it is "winning the argument" against the traditional integrative model of the European Union's development. On other occasions, confusingly, it prefers to present itself as the lone voice of reason against the almost universal European impetus to abandon the nation state in the pursuit of an economically irrational and institutionally outmoded project of political integration.

Against this background, it might have been expected that British public opinion would be at best unenthusiastic about the European Union's increasingly ambitious agenda for external and defence policy. Indeed, some such concerns began to surface in the British discussion of the European Constitutional Treaty before the French and Dutch referendums in 2005. Many of the Treaty's opponents in the United Kingdom were particularly critical of the new post of "European Foreign Minister." If there had been a British referendum on the Constitutional Treaty, much controversy would certainly have centred on this issue, with the Treaty's adversaries claiming that the new minister was a dangerous building-block for a European foreign policy, a European government and a European state. This argument would certainly have persuaded some British voters to reject the Constitutional Treaty. There would of course have been a peculiar irony in this outcome. The designation "European Foreign Minister" greatly overstated the role of the man or woman who was to succeed the present High Representative for External Affairs, Javier Solana. The Constitutional Treaty made clear in all its other provisions that the European Union would continue to act in its foreign and defence policies essentially on an intergovernmental, and not on an institutionally integrated basis. This is a political system altogether more congenial to the United Kingdom than the powerful integrative mechanisms which support most of the European Union's internal activities. Nor is Britain entirely isolated in advocating this intergovernmental approach to foreign and defence issues. France has always had some sympathy for intergovernmentalism in these areas, and the powerful integrationist impulse which used to come from Germany even in matters of European foreign and security policy is no longer as strong as it once was. The maintenance of the post of "High Representative" in the "Reform Treaty" is a telling symbol of the unwillingness of the European Union's member states to move significantly further in the "communitarisation" of their activities in the foreign policy field. What is true for foreign policy is even more demonstrably true for defence policy. The inchoate concept of "structured co-operation" in military matters, foreseen by the Constitutional and Reform Treaties is very clearly an arrangement by and for national governments, and not necessarily for all or even a majority of those member states that currently comprise the European Union. If the question of "structured co-operation" does become a controversial one in the British debate, the British government will be able to give an account of its workings highly reassuring to the British public. Indeed, the British government is likely to set about giving this account with more energy and enthusiasm than it has sometimes shown in the past in its advocacy of the European Union and its policies.

In truth, the British government sees European foreign and more particularly European security policy as the guarantee that it will never be entirely marginalised within the European Union. It will be many years before Britain joins the euro or becomes a full member of the Schengen area. As the Justice and Home Affairs pillar of the European Union has become less intergovernmental in its workings, so the United Kingdom has extended its scope to choose whether or not it will participate in new legislative initiatives bearing on the Union's internal security. The image of the United Kingdom as a "semi-detached" member of the European Union is one gaining credibility and resonance with other member states of the Union. When there is speculation about the Union's dividing itself in the medium term between an "outer" and an "inner" tier, few observers doubt that Britain will be a prime candidate to lead the "outer" tier.

Such speculation is not welcome to the British government. Until now, it has manoeuvred remarkably successfully to remain somewhere near the centre of the European Union, an organisation in the most important activities of which it only fitfully participates and the underlying institutional philosophy of which it rejects. The rejection of the Constitutional Treaty in France and the Netherlands, combined with the political stagnation following these referendums, gave some consolation to those in the British government who hoped that the momentum of the Union's institutional integration had finally been halted. The rapidity with which the new French President, working closely with Mrs. Merkel, has now broken the logjam which his compatriots did so much to create, will have taken many by surprise in London. Not for the first time, British politicians and officials underestimated the determination and energy with which their continental colleagues pursue the European institutional questions which alternately bore, irritate and offend the self-absorbed British political establishment. Foreign and defence policy will be powerful cards in the hand of any British government seeking to build a European Union of "variable geometry." A European foreign policy, and even more a European defence policy without the United Kingdom would have little global credibility for any foreseeable future. The United Kingdom's leading role in these areas will to some extent, it is hoped in London, compensate for British reticence in many other central areas of European development.

Nor, in the long term, need the supposed "special relationship" of the United Kingdom with the United States of

America pose any insuperable barrier to a full British role in European foreign and defence policy. The events in and concerning Iraq over the past five years have tried to destruction the policy whereby the highest aspiration of any British government was to act as European advocate of American policies. It is noticeable that the new British Prime Minister is now, albeit carefully and indirectly, attempting to differentiate British positions from those of the United States. Particularly striking in this context was a speech given in Washington soon after Mr. Brown became Prime Minister by the British Minister for Overseas Development, Douglas Alexander. In this speech, Mr. Alexander, who is regarded as a confidant of Mr. Brown's, delivered an enthusiastic eulogy of the virtues of "soft power" and the importance of relying in external policy upon the use of a wide range of policy instruments. Although he did not specifically contrast in this context European and American attitudes, his American audience cannot have failed to note that the tone and rhetoric of this speech emphatically came from Venus rather than from Mars.

Indeed, there seems some reason to believe that Gordon Brown may wish to rebalance British foreign policy away from its recent Atlanticist preoccupations. In so doing, he would be returning to the tradition of British diplomacy which saw the United Kingdom as a bridge between the United States and continental Europe, rather than the American "Trojan horse in Europe" of Gaullist stereotype. There is today a real opportunity for the United Kingdom's partners in the European Union to take advantage of this potential turning point in the orientation of British foreign and defence policy. It is well known that Mr. Brown played a decisive role in ensuring that Britain would not and probably will not join the euro during his time in office. But before he became Chancellor of the Exchequer in 1997, Mr. Brown had an unambiguously pro-European reputation, which he has arguably sacrificed in the past decade for reasons of domestic political advantage rather than from any fundamental shift of political philosophy. Given the domestic political disaster which British support for American policy in Iraq represented for Mr. Blair, it would be entirely logical for Mr. Brown to give a much more European colouring to his foreign policy than did his predecessor. It will be important that he receives encouragement to do so from his peers in the European Council. For the Federal Trust, an essentially intergovernmental European foreign and security policy obviously cannot comprise the definitive answer to the problems and challenges Europe faces on the world stage. But it is certainly better than no European foreign and security policy. It may be that in the longer term the United Kingdom's government will once again find itself confronted with unwelcome choices arising from the eventual "communitarisation" of European foreign and defence policy. But that day is a long way off. It is unlikely ever to be a real problem for Mr. Brown. Mr. Alexander, who is twenty years younger than Mr. Brown, is a much more likely candidate to have to wrestle with such a dilemma. Those who live longest will know most.

The future of European Security and Defence Policy: towards a European Army

By Angelica Schwall-Düren and Fabian Hemker

The idea and plans for a European army have been introduced to public discourse as early as the 1940s and 1950s. The Pleven Plan, presented to the French parliament in 1950, called for the creation of a European army, controlled by a European Council of Defence Ministers, a European Defence Minister, and a Supreme Allied Commander in time of conflict. Furthermore, the Pleven Plan included a European defence budget and a European arms procurement process. But the plan faced several obstacles, most notably its rejection by the French parliament in 1954. Thus, European capitals agreed on the establishment of the European Coal and Steel Community (ECSC), instead. But the ambitions to build a European army and a European Political Community (EPC) have not been successful as yet.

Almost 60 years after the EDC's demise, calls for a European army have risen again. Kurt Beck – chairman of the Social Democratic Party of Germany (SPD) – proposed in 2006 the establishment of integrated European forces that should lead to a European Security and Defence Union in the long run. Furthermore, the draft Party Programme of the SPD demands the development of a European army under the umbrella of the European Union (EU) by continuing the coalescence of national armies.

This essay addresses some questions that need to be answered before a decision about a European army can be made:

- What are the security and foreign policy interests of the EU that could and should be pursued by an EU army?
- What are the threats the EU faces today?
- How can the EU tackle them with a European army?
- In short: does the EU in fact need an army and if so, what for?

EU security interests
Germany's territorial security is not at danger and will remain so for the foreseeable future because war is no longer a political means in Europe since 1991 at the latest. NATO and the EU – more and more since the end of the Cold War – played and still play an important role in building a stable and peaceful Europe. Yet, stability in Europe does not imply that Germany and Europe do not need a security policy. Due to its wealth Germany is one of a few states in the world able to allocate the means for successful conflict prevention and conflict resolution. But the conduct of foreign and security policy by the German Emperor and Hitler has led many German Social Democrats to be sceptical towards any German foreign and security policy openly referring to national security interests. Moreover, many Social Democrats see themselves as pacifists and oppose any form of uses of force. This attitude, however, cannot stand the test of time. First, it ignores that foreign and security policy of any democracy must serve the interests of its citizens. Second, the social democratic principle to conduct a policy of peace comprises to support peace by appropriate means that can serve this end – including military means. It has to be stressed that the promotion of peace, democracy and human rights must not include regime change by military intervention.

However, Germany and the EU have a responsibility to contribute to peace and prosperity in a world that is getting increasingly interdependent. The German Security Policy White Paper of 2006 states "preventing regional crises and conflicts that could affect Germany's security and to contribute to conflict resolution" as one of the country's security interests. The European neighbourhood is of specific importance. The serious effects intrastate conflicts can have on neighbouring states is shown in the Sudan-Chad border region – though not only there. Conflict prevention and conflict resolution in the European neighbourhood must therefore be a priority of German security policy. Moreover, Germany is interested in securing its energy supply and trade routes. These interests are not limited spatially but embrace the world as a whole – be it the Middle East, the Black Sea region or Central Asia. Finally, the terrorist attacks of Madrid and London have shown that states hosting terrorists are an indirect threat to the security of European citizens. Germany is, therefore, interested in stable states that do not support terrorism.

The EU's security interests, as defined in article 11 TEU, are similar to Germany's: "to preserve peace and strengthen international security in accordance with the principles of the United Nations Charter", and to "develop and consolidate democracy and the rule of law, and respect for human rights and fundamental freedoms." The mandate of the Intergovernmental Conference that will adopt the reform treaty further clarifies these objectives (to-be article 3 para. 4): the EU shall uphold and promote its values and interests, contribute to the protection of its citizens as well as to peace and security, sustainable development, solidarity and the protection of human rights. The EU shall further international law and respect the principles of the UN Charter. In 1999, the EU integrated the so-called Petersberg Tasks of the Western European Union (WEU) into the TEU. These tasks form a catalogue of operations, the EU should be able to conduct, e.g. humanitarian and rescue tasks or peacekeeping and peacemaking.

Finally, the European Security Strategy (ESS) of December 2003 calls on Europe to be "ready to share in the responsibility for global security and in building a better world." To defend its security and to promote its values the EU has three strategic objectives: it must address the threats, foster security in its neighbourhood, and contribute to global governance based on an effective multilateralism. Neither Germany nor the EU can lock out all conflicts of the contemporary world. The attacks mentioned above have shown this most direly. Even the immediate European neighbourhood is not safe enough for the EU to renounce military means.

UN demand for European military and civil-military means is strong and will remain so in the future as the UN does not have its own troops for peace operations. Since its creation in 1999 the EU has conducted 17 peace operations (civilian, military and civil-military) under its European Defence and Security Policy (ESDP), for example in the Balkans, the Palestinian Territories and the Democratic Republic of Congo. To live up to its obligations, the EU must have capabilities that enforce peace if preventive action fails. Any deployment of EU troops for peace operations must serve European interests, respect European values and has to be eligible, necessary and appropriate to achieve the peace operation's objective.

Regional conflicts
According to the ESS regional conflicts and failed or failing states are threats to European interests. The collapse of Yugoslavia in the 1990s revealed European powerlessness to end violent conflicts even in its immediate neighbourhood. The EU has not been able to prevent the ethnic cleansings in Bosnia and Kosovo without help from NATO. As a result, thousands of people in collapsing Yugoslavia have been killed and many more tried to take refuge in neighbouring European countries. And the Balkan wars have not been the only deadly conflicts during the 1990s: about four million people – most of them civilians – died in wars around the world since 1990. Violence and its effects

have caused tens of millions of refugees to pose a global challenge for the EU because asylum capabilities in the EU member states are limited and humanitarian crises are hard to bear for the European public.

European interests threatened by failed states
Undoubtedly there are many places in the world that are not secure, not democratic, not governed by the rule of law, and lacking guaranteed human rights and fundamental freedoms. In 2007, 17 major conflicts are happening; 20 states are so unstable that they have to be viewed as failed states. In 2006, presidential elections in the Democratic Republic of Congo – currently one of the weakest states in the world – have taken place only because the EU had sent troops to the capital Kinshasa. Non-state actors like the Djanjaweed in Sudan are increasingly prominent in conflicts but the capacity of the international community to hold them in control is limited. The EU and its member states are involved in nine peace operations with more than 8,000 troops and police officers as yet. And the UN increasingly calls for EU-support when a weak state collapses and violence escalates.

Worldwide Terrorism, organized crime and weapons of mass destruction
Besides regional conflicts and state failure, the ESS identifies three additional threats: terrorism, the proliferation of weapons of mass destruction, and organised crime. Terrorism and organised crime are often side-effects of failed and failing states. They mostly flourish where regional conflicts are going on and effective governmental structures are absent. For example, poppy cultivation in Afghanistan is a result of a weak state unable to fight the Afghan drug business effectively and unable to provide alternative ways of securing farmers' income. Today, 90 per cent of heroin traded in Europe originates from Afghanistan. Violent conflicts are often financed from revenues generated by organised crime. The best strategy to counter terrorism and organised crime is to address their causes –

conflict, poverty, hunger, diseases and a lack of alternative income opportunities. Although European military means can contribute to end violent conflicts, it must be stressed that the use of force by the EU can only complement the manifold European efforts to establish functioning governments which in turn will be able to fight terrorism and organised crime themselves.

Finally, the third threat named in the ESS – the proliferation of weapons of mass destruction (WMD) – as well as small arms and light weapons (SALW) – must be addressed by international law. Therefore, multilateral treaties, e.g. the Non-Proliferation Treaty and its protocols and the EU strategies against the Proliferation of WMD and against illicit accumulation and trafficking of SALW and their ammunition are the best way to tackle this threat. The proliferation of weapons of mass destruction and SALW cannot not be countered by military means. Thus, the only threats that can and should be countered by military means are violent conflicts in areas of vital interest to the EU.

Part of the Answer: a European Army

The European powerlessness during the Balkan wars has led to the creation of the ESDP under the German Council Presidency in 1999. In fact ESDP is necessary to implement the Petersberg tasks. In less than a decade the EU institutionalised this policy by establishing the Political and Security Committee, the Military Committee, the Military Staff and the Civil Crisis Management Committee under the guise of the Council. With its battle groups – each consisting of 1,500 rapidly deployable troops – the EU already has a European army or at least "the beginning of a European army" as former EU operation "Artemis" force commander and French General Christian Damay stated. Just as the question of an EU *finalité* has not yet been answered, the final shape of ESDP has not yet been determined. Thus, Former Deputy Minister of Defence, Walther Stützle, recommended the EU should explicitly set itself the target of a European army rather than entering further long-winded procedures without an ultimate goal.

Duplication, decoupling, discrimination?

First, a European army would be able to conduct operations NATO does not want to conduct. EUFOR Congo is a good example, even though the preventive deterrence operation has shown that the EU needs to improve its operational planning, logistics and technical capabilities. Second, the EU would gain more options – political and military – to influence global politics against the background of its objectives. Egon Bahr recently summarised this argument by saying that Europe's weight would grow if it had its own, independently serviceable army at its disposal. Third, budgetary strains prevent EU member states from duplicating NATO capabilities. NATO is interested in strong European military capabilities that strengthen its European pillar and satisfy transatlantic demands of better burden sharing.

A European Army would not decouple ESDP from NATO because even the TEU determines that ESDP has to respect member states obligations to the alliance – ESDP must be separable but not separate from NATO. Moreover, the principle of a single set of forces for ESDP and NATO inhibits decoupling. Finally, the Intergovernmental Conference will presumably adopt a resolution emphasising that CFSP does not affect "the responsibilities of the Member states, as they currently exist, for the formulation and conduct of their foreign policy nor of their national representation in third countries and international organisations."

Nor would a European army discriminate countries being members of NATO but not of the EU or vice versa. There will always be non-participation of some countries in NATO and the EU due to the two institutions' nature – transatlantic and European, respectively. The EU will definitely not "go global" and even if NATO becomes a global institution it will nevertheless discriminate against authoritarian regimes. Hence, some discrimination will be inevitable and the UN will remain the only global institution.

The European battle groups: beginning or end of a European army?

The European battle groups are not a sufficient means for the EU to reach its security objectives. Until now, the battle groups are combined, but not joined, forces, i.e. they consist of multinational contributions, yet are largely restricted to land forces. At the moment, air and naval forces need to be attached if needed. If the battle groups remain restricted to land forces, any European crisis management capability will be restricted accordingly. To solve these deficiencies, Germany and France – supported by the UK, the Netherlands and Belgium – have proposed an "EU Maritime Reaction Concept" in 2004 and a "Rapid Reaction Air Initiative" in 2005. The implementation of both proposals is under way and will contribute to solving these shortcomings.

A European army: gain or loss for the EU?

EU Member states command about 1.7 million troops but only a fraction of them –50,000-60,000 – can be used in parallel to fulfil the Petersberg tasks. As Europe does not need large conventional forces to counter a possible Soviet attack any more, the current European force level is not necessary to serve European interests. Thus, it is questionable if all member states in fact need land, sea and air forces. Against this background EU member states agree about the necessity to transform their armies towards developing rapid reaction forces that can be deployed rapidly. A military division of labour and an integration of forces would boost European military capacities and capabilities at the same time. But EU means for conflict prevention and conflict resolution will remain limited even after the EU establishes an army in this way as the EU is not able to deploy its capabilities to all places of crises. An updated ESS should therefore answer the question if it is possible to develop criteria with which the EU can comprehensibly decide when and where to engage with which means. For German Social Democrats it is – and will remain – important that parliamentary participation in decision-making on every single armed operation is guaranteed. There has to be an equivalent to the German Parliament's right of prior approval (*Parlamentsvorbehalt*) for operations of a European army.

In addition to the unnecessary high number of troops, much European money is spent for defence procurement in a non-cost-efficient way. Member states' combined defence budgets amount to about 200 billion per annum but most of their capabilities do not meet today's challenges. A European army could contribute to a division of military tasks, mainstreaming procurement, and pooling military development and research efforts. The division of labour in the military sector could lead to a better capabilities-to-money-ratio and greater capabilities at the same time. British and French nuclear weapons will neither be part of the procurement process nor part of ESDP in general because, first, it is unlikely that the UK and France will agree to shared control over their national nuclear stockpiles with other EU member states. Secondly, a European army does not need nuclear weapons to fulfil the Petersberg tasks.

Fears of a European army leading to a division within the EU if realised by way of a "Two-speed Europe" with only interested member states participating must be encountered by saying that the establishment of a European army formed by all 27 EU member states is unlikely. European integration already knows different paces as the Schengen Agreement and monetary integration show. Even ESDP itself is not an all-EU endeavour, Denmark's deliberate reserve being a case in point. This method of integration has strengthened the EU rather than dividing it. In this vain, European military integration through enhanced cooperation will in fact deepen the economic and political Union.

Primacy of civilian conflict prevention and conflict resolution
Against the background of the EU's commitment to promote progress in the world, the Union is bound to address the causes of conflicts. Thus ESDP also contains civilian instruments. But military means can be necessary because security is a

precondition for development. It is necessary to guarantee the safety of those people who try to help weak states develop. Poverty, hunger, malnutrition and diseases can only be fought if there is a minimum of security. Civilian conflict management capabilities are part of every sustainable conflict resolution effort. The EU emphasis of civilian means will not be changed by the establishment of a European army. Quite the contrary, European soft power will be developed further as civilian efforts are bolstered by armed forces providing security.

Germany and the EU face threats and challenges to their security interests and obligations that can only be countered by effective and efficient military means. The aim of EU security policy is to prevent war and not let it occur. But if war occurs the EU must be capable and willing to use military means to end it and help building sustainable societies. A European army would contribute to this.

Hanging Together or Hanging Separately? The EU3, the United States and Iran's Nuclear Quest

By Sebastian Harnisch

Iran's nuclear program has become the centre of international attention, since the IAEA discovered in 2003 that Iran had been breaching its "Comprehensive Safeguards Agreement" (CSA) over an extended period of 18 years. As a consequence, starting in August 2003 the French, German and British Foreign Ministers (E3), who were joined in autumn 2004 by Javier Solana (EU3), sought to restore international confidence in the peaceful nature of the Iranian nuclear program. Yet, the European mediation encountered a serious setback in August 2005 when Tehran restarted its uranium enrichment activities after almost two years of suspension, thereby drawing potentially closer to a military application. As a result, the EU3 shifted gear from mediation to coalition building for a sanctions-based strategy.[1]

In January 2006, the former EU3 minilateralism was joined by the United States, China and Russia and rechristened the EU3+3. Up to now, this new format has failed to stop Iran's pursuit of a full nuclear fuel cycle capacity, i.e. the ability to enrich uranium and reprocess plutonium. The sanctions imposed in Security Council Resolutions 1737 and 1747 have not altered Tehran's course. Instead, hard line President Ahmadinejad has tried to inflame Iranian nationalism by making excessive claims about Iran's technical prowess. While this Iranian strategy may eventually backfire, it has already abated the room of manoeuvre for a diplomatic settlement considerably.

In this context, the following article explores the question of which lessons can be drawn from the EU3+3 with Iran experience. Originally, the E3 and EU-3 sought to resolve the conflict over Tehran's suspicious civilian program by restoring confidence in its peaceful nature through suspension of sensitive activities and providing transparency concerning its past transgressions. However, that mediation strategy was doomed to failure because it was inconsistent with basic assumptions about successful mediation in international conflict. Threats and benefits do not, as a rule, generate a stable conflict resolution, if these are not supported by all the major powers concerned, in this case the United States.[2] Secondly, the EU-3+3 paid insufficient attention to the underspecification of Art IV (Non-proliferation Treaty) that is the inalienable right to engage in full fuel cycle activities by non-nuclear weapon states. In particular, the EU-3 did not forge a legally binding consensus on how this norm should be interpreted in the case of an IAEA member state that is in non-compliance with its Comprehensive Safeguards Agreement. Thirdly, and more recently, the EU3+3 failed to understand the internal regime dynamics in Tehran with regard to suspension of uranium enrichment as a precondition for a comprehensive settlement.

The argument proceeds in three steps: The first section briefly touches upon the achievements of the EU-3, i.e. suspension, coherence among the major powers concerned, and the restraint imposed/exercised by third parties. The second section is focused on the failures, in order to learn from past experience. The final section concludes that the EU3 and Washington must forge a more consistent diplomatic strategy based on security insurances, limited compromises and strong verification mechanisms, to successfully test Tehran's willingness to cooperate or to lay the groundwork for more and serious economic sanctions. Thus, if the EU3+3 fail to hang together more closely, in the end they may hang separately.

Achievements

The first and most important achievement of the E3 has been the so called Tehran Declaration. Although this was only a one-sided declaration by the E3, it successfully persuaded Iran to sign and implement the additional protocol, to commit itself to answer all outstanding questions with regard to its nuclear past, and most importantly, to temporarily suspend sensitive full-fuel cycle activities. This was all the more significant because the E3 backing by the EU and from the US was limited at the time. In addition, when the Iranians started to back-pedal on their suspension commitment in spring 2004, the E3, through a harshly worded but consensual IAEA Board of Governors' resolution, gained the necessary international backing to press Tehran a bit further. In the resulting Paris Agreement, the now EU-3 tried to reinstate a more comprehensive suspension and effectively succeeded in persuading Iran to postpone enrichment activities for another year.

Some critics of the EU-3 mediation effort argue that suspension was a price the Iranians were happy to pay at the time, because suspension was crucial to persuade the E3 to keep the Iranian case out of the UN Security Council and to complete their uranium conversion program:

"While we were talking with the Europeans in Tehran, we were installing equipment in parts of the facility in Isfahan... in fact by creating a calm environment, we were able to complete the work in Isfahan. Today, we can covert yellowcake into UF4 and UF6, and this is a very important matter."[3]

Delaying Security Council referral while advancing its technical capacity may well have been part of the Iranian calculus, as the interview with Iran's chief nuclear negotiator Rowhani suggests. But three objections to this assertion can be raised: first, technically the Iranians most probably did not advance their enrichment effort as fast as they would have done without suspension; secondly, suspension could also be read as a European delaying tactic. After the Iraq split, the E3 were neither willing nor able to refer Iran in late 2003 to the UN SC anyway. Thirdly, the Rohani interview claim can also be read as trying to cover up the domestic struggle inside Iran between those factions that were willing to take the Europeans/Americans head-on and the more cautious faction that thought that a negotiated settlement was still possible.[4] In sum, the lesson learned here is that the E3 had been able to build a growing international coalition to prevent the conflict from escalating earlier by considerably slowing down the Iranian enrichment effort.[5]

The second major achievement of the E3 initiative was the growing coherence between the E3, EU-3 and finally the EU3 + 3 position and the signatories of the NPT. To begin with, in late summer 2003 neither all EU member states nor the Bush administration as a whole supported the E3 publicly or privately. While some European governments suspected another attempt to form a *directoire* (after the 2002 London dinner), the Pentagon, National Security Council and Vice-Presidency were highly sceptical if not hostile vis-à-vis negotiations with the Iranian regime. And yet, in the months to follow the E3 were able to forge an ever more coherent international coalition. Starting with the U.S. Secretary of State Powell, the Big Three persuaded most members of the IAEA Board of Governors to support the E3 mediation effort in 2004 and finally coopted Condoleezza Rice and Stephen Hadley in the winter of 2004. As a consequence, the EU-3 tabled an enhanced negotiation proposal that contained some limited lifting of US sanctions in August 2005.

After Iran had restarted uranium enrichment in January 2006, the EU-3 were joined by Russia and China. Most notably, and despite earlier vocal opposition, Russia supported UN SC 1737 and 1747 that ban, amongst other things, technical and financial assistance to Iran's enrichment, reprocessing, heavy-water and ballistic missile programs. In addition, while the resolution did not touch Russian-Iranian cooperation in finalising the LWR plant in Busher, Moscow subsequently did suspend its support for the project. In sum, the E3 proved its capacity as a coalition builder while maintaining some of its credibility as a mediator between that coalition and Iran.

The last major achievement of the EU-3 and the EU-3+3 minilateralism is the continued restraint by third parties, most importantly Israel but also Saudi-Arabia and Egypt. Some policymakers and pundits argue that Iran can be deterred from attacking its neighbours, but it is hard to imagine any Israeli government agreeing. As a consequence, one conclusion is that past and current Israeli governments have not used pre-emption, as in the case of the Osirak reactor, at least in part because they hoped that the EU-3 (+3) may ultimately succeed in resolving the conflict peacefully. Of course, several considerations factor in the Israeli decision-making process: private US security assurances, the technical status of the Iranian program, the ongoing asymmetrical conflict with Iran's proxy Hezbollah in Lebanon and the stability of the governing coalition in Israel itself. However, it is reasonable to conclude that Israel as well as many other countries were pleased that the E3 prevented a rapid escalation during the period from 2003 to 2005. The same "buying time" argument also applies to Saudi-Arabia and Egypt, because both have ambitions for regional leadership and a troubled history with the Shiite Islamic regime in Tehran. In the case of an open Iranian nuclear weapons capacity, these states would then face a very difficult choice. Either they acquiesce to a nuclear Iran or they will have to balance that capacity through internal means, i.e. going nuclear themselves, or external means, i.e. acquiring security assurances from a nuclear weapons state such as the US. As both options would involve substantial domestic or foreign costs for the regimes, governments in Cairo and Riyadh supported the suspension negotiated and extended by the EU-3. In addition, as most Arab states are weary, sceptical or even hostile about US motives in Iraq and the Gulf, Arab neighbours of Iran tend to appreciate the moderating influence of the EU-3 vis-à-vis Washington.

As a consequence, the EU-3+3 through their mediation effort have so far blocked a nuclear domino effect. Notably, starting with the E3, the EU has proven its crisis prevention capacity in the non-proliferation field where its formal competences have been very limited and divisions between non-nuclear weapon states and nuclear weapon states have prevented joint actions and policies in the past.

Failures

Despite these important successes, the EU-3 + 3 initiative has obviously failed to stop the evolving Iranian capacity to enrich uranium, which may be used for military purposes in the medium-term future.[6]

The most important deficit of the EU3+3 initiative has been a lack policy consistency as a precondition for successful mediation. It is worth noting that the E3 got off the ground only after the USG rejected an Iranian offer (through the Swiss government) for a comprehensive settlement. Hence, the E3 filled a vacuum created by the Bush administration that was split in early 2003 between a faction of policy makers who were willing to consider bilateral talks and a majority faction opposed to it. Since then, the EU-3 has been able to slightly shift that balance in Washington's Iran policy.[7] But several actions taken by the Bush administration have compromised the EU3's ability to formulate a consistent negotiating position: first, despite repeated Iranian calls, the Bush administration could not agree upon security assurances for the Islamic Republic, even on a contingent basis; second, by negotiating a nuclear cooperation with India, which legitimises a non-NPT member state to pursue nuclear weapons production (with active US support) and hold considerable fissile material outside international safeguards, Washington has made it much harder for the EU-3 to argue that

Iran, as an NPT member state without nuclear weapons, must suspend or even forego uranium enrichment and plutonium reprocessing which it had already agreed to place under IAEA safeguards a long time ago. Third, while supporting the EU3 negotiations in general, the Bush Administration has stepped up its diplomatic and military efforts to isolate Iran in the Gulf region. Trying to form an alliance of moderate Arab countries, i.e. Egypt, Jordan, Saudi-Arabia and the Gulf monarchies, arming them with modern weapons systems, ratcheting up the economic pressure on Iran, funding Iranian opposition groups in exile and deploying additional military capacities to the region, may well be a rational and appropriate course of action considering Iran's involvement in Iraq and Lebanon. And yet, it is plausible that these measures did not improve the chances of a negotiated settlement when taken together with the rejection of security assurances for the regime in Tehran. In sum, the lesson to be drawn is that while the E3 was able start a mediation effort and form an impressive consensus, the EU3 simply cannot guarantee that the United States will not take advantage of Iran's disarmament, if it were to happen, to pursue regime change by force or subversion.[8]

The second major deficit of the EU3+3 effort deals with the ambiguous nature of the norm in Art. IV. To begin with, in both the Tehran statement and Paris Agreement, the EU3 agreed that the Iranian suspension of enrichment and reprocessing were voluntary and non-legally binding. Yet during the negotiations the EU3 also stressed that uranium enrichment and conversion as well as plutonium reprocessing activities were not "normal activities" in the case of Iran, because it had concealed a lot of activities from the IAEA that could be used to produce nuclear weapons.[9] In short, in the EU3 reading of Article IV, 1, the inalienable right of all NPT parties to carry out peaceful nuclear activities must be curtailed in cases of non-compliance. The deficit of the EU-3's approach lies in the inability or unwillingness to specify the concrete terms of this curtailment between 2003 and 2006 while the Iranians lacked the technical capacity to enrich uranium. In November 2004, Teheran requested the exemption of 20 centrifuges from the voluntary suspension while reportedly offering to put off uranium hexafluoride (UF6) production. In spring 2005, Tehran requested permission to run a 64-centrifuge cascade in exchange for putting off industrial scale enrichment for 10 years. In spring 2006, Iran may have settled for an extended freeze of uranium enrichment with only a 164-centrifuge cascade running.[10] Thus, between 2003 and 2006 there were various opportunities to limit Iran's enrichment effort. While this was certainly a less desirable outcome than the zero-enrichment position taken, zero enrichment, as the mother of all options, has now been overtaken by the technical progress Iran has made.

As a consequence, the EU-3+3 have raised the legal bar above which Iran may restart its proliferation sensitive activities at some point in the future. Security Council Resolutions 1696 (31 July 2006), 1737 (23 December 2006), 1747 (24 March 2007) require Iran (under Chapt. VII) to suspend all "enrichment-related and reprocessing activities, including research and development and work on all heavy-water related projects, including the construction of a research reactor moderated by heavy water" (i.e. Arak).[11] A negotiated settlement has become much harder, because, amongst other things, these legally binding council demands require another council resolution by the council permitting Iran to restart enrichment and reprocessing. Iran has voiced deep scepticism that the Security Council would ever permit it to recommence these sensitive activities.[12]

Third, now that Iran has at least partially mastered the process to enrich uranium[13], it is implausible that Tehran will agree to a zero enrichment position, even on a temporary basis: First, there is a broad domestic consensus in Iran that enrichment (and reprocessing) is an inalienable right that cannot and has not been forfeited by Iran. Second, while some policy makers, Rohani and Rafsanjani, have suggested that they may agree to another temporary curtailment of proliferation prone activities, the conservative faction around Ahmadinejad has ruled this out.[14] Finally, as the conservative forces lost considerable domestic support in the last elections due to their poor economic performance, they are even more inclined to use external conflicts to improve their domestic political standing. The seizure of British soldiers in the Gulf is a case in point here. In sum, and considering the latest compromise proposal in the Larijani-Solana talks in February and April 2007, this reading of the domestic regime dynamics in Tehran suggests that a moratorium on additional centrifuge instalments seems plausible but a "double suspension" – suspension of all enrichment activities in exchange for the suspension of sanctions[15] – during multilateral talks over an extended period will be much more difficult to implement.

Conclusions: Lessons to be drawn

What does this analysis suggest for the future course of action? First, the EU3 has bought some time for negotiations, but it was ill-prepared to strike a deal. The EU3 simply did not have the "negotiation power" with all essential positive and negative incentives at its disposal. The lesson for transatlantic cooperation here is: either the EU3 and Washington will hang together even more closely or they will hang separately when diplomacy fails. As a minimum, the EU3+3 need at least Washington's approval of security assurances for the regime. Second, the other important factor to bolster transatlantic cooperation is the ability of the Bush administration to forge a consistent course on Iran. This would limit Iran's ability to manipulate public opinion and the policies of the non-aligned movement and it would strengthen Europe's confidence in the Bush administration's decision making process. So far that has not been the case. Third, Iran's technical progress since August 2005 has considerably inflated the price for a negotiated settlement. The EU3+3 sanctions-based strategy may succeed in stopping that progress through Security Council action, but external sanctions will not roll back the Iranian enrichment effort. Hence, zero-enrichment is no longer a viable policy. The EU3+3 should negotiate "limited enrichment options" with extensive safeguards and sequential steps to rebuild trust in Iran's nuclear dealings.

Endnotes

1   See Harnisch, Sebastian (2007): "Minilateral coalition building and transatlantic cooperation: the E3/EU-3 Iran initiative", European Security, vol.16, no.1, pp. 1-27.

2   See Moore, Christopher (2003): The Mediation Process. Pratcial Strategies for Resolving Conflict, 3rd. Rev. Ed., San Francisco, CA, pp.193-194.

3   See Rohani, Hassan (2003): "Beyond the Challenges Facing Iran and the IAEA Concerning the Nuclear Dossier", in: Rahbord (2005), translated by FBIS and available at: http://www.armscontrolwonk.com/file_download/30 [13.06.2007].

4   See Smyth, Gareth (2006): "Fundamentalists, Pragmatists, and the rights of Nations: Iranian Politics and Nuclear Confrontation", Washington, DC. The Century Foundation, http://www.tcf.org/publications/internationalaffairs/smyth_iran.pdf [17.06.2007].

5   See Fitzpatrick, Mark (2007): "Can Iran's Nuclear Capability be kept latent?", Survival, vol.49, no.1,p.35.

6   See Albright, David (2006): "When could Iran get the Bomb?", Bulletin of Atomic Scientists,vol.62, no.4, pp. 26-33.

7   See Leverett, Flynt (2006): "Dealing with Tehran: Assessing U.S. Diplomatic Options toward Iran", New York: The Century Foundation, http://www.tcf.org/publications/internationalaffairs/leverett_diplomatic.pdf [17.06.2007].

8   See Martin, Curtis H. (2007): ""Good Cop/Bad Cop" as a model for non-proliferation diplomacy toward North Korea and Iran", Nonproliferation Review, vol.14, no.1, p.82.

9   See Harnisch, Sebastian/Linden, Ruth (2005): "Iran and Nuclear Proliferation – Europe's slow burning diplomatic crisis", German Foreign Policy in Dialogue, vol. 6, no.17, pp. 44-54, http://www.deutsche-aussenpolitik.de/newsletter/issue17.pdf [17.06.2007].

10 See Fitzpatrick, Mark (2007): "Can Iran's Nuclear Capability be kept latent?", Survival, vol.49, no.1, p.50.

11 See Persbo, Andreas (2007): "Thinking inside the box: exploring legal approaches to build confidence in Iran's nuclear programme", Vertic Research Reports, p.11, http://www.vertic.org/publications/ VM7.pdf [13.06.2007].

12 See Acton, James/Joana Little (2007): "The Use of Voluntary safeguards to build trust in states' nuclear programmes: the case of Iran", Vertic Research Reports, p.11, http://www.vertic.org/ publications/VM8.pdf [13.06.2007].

13 For a current critical assessment see Persbo, Andreas (2007): "Iranian Centrifuge construction", http://verificationthoughts.blogspot.com/ 2007/06/iranian-centrifuge-construction.html [17.06.2007].

14 See International Crisis Group (2006): "Iran: Is there a Way out of the Nuclear Impasse?", Middle East Report, no. 51, pp.8-10, http://www.crisisgroup.org/library/documents/middle_east___ north_africa/iraq_iran_gulf/51_an_is_there_a_way_out_of_the_ nuclear_impasse.pdf [17.06.2007].
   See Kane, Chen (2006): "Nuclear Decision Making in Iran: A rare Glimpse", Middle East Brief, Brandeis University, no.5, http://www.brandeis.edu/centers/crown/publications/MEB/MEB5.pdf [13.06.2007].

15 See Samore, Gary (2007): "Iran's Nuclear Programme. Can diplomacy succeed", Strategic Comments, vol.13, no.3, p.2, http://www.cfr.org/content/publications/attachments/ Iran%20Diplomacy%20Samore.pdf [13.06.2007].

Conclusion

By Stephen Haseler and Jeannette Ladzik

There have been a number of important developments and accomplishments in ESDP during the German presidency as Annegret Bendiek and Brendan Donnelly point out in their articles. Especially the civil component of ESDP, a major focus of Germany's presidency, has been evolved in the first half of 2007. At the ESDP conference in Berlin on 29-30 January 2007, new ideas for restructuring the Council Secretariat were discussed. The option of creating a Civilian Operations Commander has received particular support. In June 2007, the EU Council of Ministers agreed to introduce the new post of a Civilian Operations Commander within the Council Secretariat supported by a team called Civilian Planning and Conduct Capability that he/she will lead. Future Joint Actions will put the Civilian Operations Commander in the command chain above the Head of Mission for a civilian mission, enabling him/her to support and advise the Head of Mission.

With effect from 1 January 2007, the EU also has, besides using common NATO assets and capabilities under the Berlin-

Plus arrangement or drawing on one of the national Operational Headquarters designed by five EU member states (France, Germany, Greece, Italy and the UK), a third option for commanding, from Brussels, missions and operations of limited size. Since that date, the new EU Operations Centre within the EU Military Staff has been ready for action.

The European Council decided in December 2004 to establish a Civil-Military Cell within the EU Military Staff in Brussels and tasked it to set up an Operations Centre able to plan and to run an operation, in particular where a joint civil/military response is required and where no national Headquarters is identified. The idea of an autonomous EU military headquarters surfaced for the first time at a meeting between France, Germany, Belgium and Luxemburg during the height of the Iraq crisis. At this meeting, which became infamously known as Chocolate summit, the four states called for a nucleus capacity for planning and conducting autonomous operations without recourse to NATO to be set up in the Brussels suburb Tervuren. This proposal was rejected by most of the other EU member states. Yet after close consultation, the UK, France and Germany were able to present a paper at the EU Foreign Minister meeting in Naples in November 2003, in which they recommended the creation of a small strategic planning group with an operational dimension based in the European quarter in Brussels as well as the installation of a small permanent EU cell within NATO Headquarters SHAPE. This British-French-German deal was endorsed by the December 2003 European Council. In the second half of 2005, the Civil-Military Cell has become a reality. It has a unique configuration. For the first time, officers, diplomats, civilian experts and Council and Commission officials are brought together in a single integrated setting. The cell is divided into two parts of activity. One is the strategic planning branch which carries out contingency and advanced planning. The aim of this is to enhance the Union's capacity for rapid action. The other division is a permanent staff that oversees the planning and running of autonomous EU operations. This staff forms the core nucleus of the EU Military Staff's new Operations Centre. It is important to note that the Operations Centre is not a standing headquarters. Instead, it is a permanently available capacity to rapidly set up a headquarters for a particular operation. The Operations Centre will achieve an Initial Operating Capability, that is the ability to plan, within five days at the latest, and it will reach Full Operational Capability, that is the ability to run the operation, within twenty days. A watch-keeping capability will be established within the Operations Centre ensuring round-the-clock links with the various civilian ESDP operations and the Civilian Planning and Conduct Capability.

The idea for a Civil-Military Cell rather than a military headquarters stemmed essentially from the need to achieve a political deal with the US but also from European operational experiences and the expectation that future operation will be increasingly joined up and perhaps even joint. As Javier Solana rightly argues in his article, the combination of the use of military and civilian instruments in crisis management constitutes the strength of the EU. The world today is no longer one in which military action alone determines the outcome of conflicts. Military action must always take place within a political concept. Otherwise, it leads to impasse. The EU is able to draw on a mixture of instruments ranging from civilian and military crisis management to economic, political and institution building in a flexible joined-up way. ESDP is only one tool among these different instruments and not an end in itself. This civil-military coordination is the main added value of the EU's crisis management and distinguishes the EU from NATO. NATO is ill-designed for such coordination. Accordingly, civil-military cooperation makes the European planning capabilities a necessary duplication.

Yet, the EU's vocation as a crisis manager remains hampered by military capability related difficulties and shortfalls. For example, progress towards fulfilling the Headline Goal 2010 is patchy. At the moment, shortfalls are being assessed by comparing the actual contributions of the member states in the Force Catalogue with the Requirement Catalogue, which lists apart from the military requirements needed to fulfil the Headline Goal 2010 the remaining requirements from the Helsinki Headline Goal. The result of this process will be presented in the Progress Catalogue later in the year. At the beginning of Germany's presidency, on 1 January 2007, the EU Battlegroups were declared fully operational. Yet, doubts remain over the utility as well as the rapid deployability of the Battlegroups since they have not been deployed so far although an initial operational capability has already been obtained in 2005 and conceivable missions could have been the military operation in the Democratic Republic of the Congo during the election process. Also, according to Angelica Schwall-Düren and Fabian Hemker, Battlegroups are largely restricted to land forces. If needed, air and naval forces have to be attached. Work has therefore started on a possible revision of the EU Military Rapid Response Concept. A Food-for-Thought paper by the Tri-Presidency (Germany, Portugal and Slovenia) aims at developing procedures to generate forces rapidly and enhance the ability to conduct joint air, sea and land operations. This work will concluded by mid-2008.

The future of the EU's military capabilities depends on member states spending more on defence and most importantly, spending on the right things. European defence spending not only trails far behind that of the US but the output is also little given that for example Europe has more than two million men and women in uniform but finds it hard to deploy five per cent of its combined forces. The EU member states need to readjust their military cost structure spending less on personnel and thus more on the acquisition of new equipment and on R&D. The European Defence Agency has been set up to improve this input-output ratio.

Military expenditure also varies unevenly among the EU member states. About 80% of total EU spending and 98% of military R&D expenditure are covered by the six most important arms producing countries, the so-called LoI-states (UK, France, Germany, Italy, Spain, and Sweden). This fact however is a powerful argument in support of the proposition that the best way forward for the EU member states to increase their military capabilities would be through the greatest possible degree of defence integration. According to the European Security Strategy, "systematic use of pooled and shared assets would reduce duplications, overheads, and, in the medium-term, increase capabilities". Especially, pooling has proven attractive to some member states since it allows them to preserve national autonomy whilst generating cost-effective solutions. Specialisation in "niche" capabilities is attractive in particular for smaller European countries. The EU member states will need over the coming decade to decide what is the balance they wish to strike in the defence field between national independence and the enhanced collective capacity generated by further integration.

On the other hand, since most of the burden of developing the EU's military potency lies on a limited number of member states a "pioneer group" in ESDP could emerge. Schwall-Düren and Hemker argue for such a "Two-speed-Europe" in ESDP in their article. According to them, this method of integration has strengthened the EU rather than dividing it. Sebastian Harnisch's article also focuses on this issue by explaining the trilateral initiative of France, Germany and the UK in persuading Iran to give up its nuclear programme. So, is the creation of a *directoire* in ESDP really the way forward? It is obvious that the three big member states – France, Germany and the UK – play a decisive role in ESDP. Where they reach a compromise, for example on the Civil-Military Cell, the other member states are likely to accept it. Such cooperation however has to be informal and permeable in the sense that information for the other EU partners should be provided and EU institutions involved. Furthermore, it remains to be seen whether the group composition will not change as member states, like Italy, Spain or Poland, insist on joining.

Conclusion

The German EU presidency was successful in further developing ESDP instruments. According to High Representative Javier Solana, the EU must nevertheless continue to address efforts to enhance the interplay of civilian and military instruments, provide a new impetus to defence reform and modernisation and develop effective partnerships with other key partners and actors, such as the US, NATO and the UN. The EU must also further develop its Common Foreign and Security Policy. Most of the articles within this report deal with CFSP too. CFSP strengthens the effectiveness of ESDP. The political framework gives the Union's operations clear objectives and deep support. ESDP, on the other hand, has made CFSP more credible. It has given the EU's dialogue with third countries strength. Hence, both complement each other.

Endnotes

1   See Schmitt, Burkard (2005): "Defence Expenditure", Institute for Security Studies, p.3, http://www.iss-eu.org/esdp/11-bsdef.pdf [07.08.2007].

2   European Security Strategy: "A Secure Europe in a Better World", 12.12.2003, p.13 http://ue.eu.int/uedocs/cmsUpload/78367.pdf [07.02.2006].

3   See Solana, Javier (2007): „The quiet success of European Defence", Schlossplatz, Hertie School of Governance, p.11, http://www.consilium.europa.eu/ueDocs/cms_Data/docs/pressdata/EN/articles/93752.pdf [07.08.2007].

www.ingramcontent.com/pod-product-compliance
Lightning Source LLC
Chambersburg PA
CBHW022126280326
41933CB00007B/567